All my…

notebooks

Author represented by Tibor Kleinberg

Copyright © 2019 Valentin Hämmerle
Vali-g@gmx.at
All rights reserved.

ISBN: 9781712788202

Hello there, i am your notebook!

You might wonder why you are reading this right now.

You know, i am as alive as you are! In fact, i im kind of a reflection of you.

Also, i am very curious and i really want to get to know you and i definetly want to know what keeps you busy all day long!

No worries! I can keep secrets for myself ;-)

You chose me so that you can put everything down on paper and i chose you because you are great!
Great and interesting and you got a lot of other qualities
i would like to discover while you are writing into me.

With that being said, have fun and PLEASE don't put me aside. Keep writing! ☺

xoxo your notebook

49

82